Technique for the Advancing Pianist

An Essential Collection of Progressive Exercises and Etudes

Valerie Cisler & Maurice Hinson

FOREWORD

This book is designed to serve as a technical skills instructional and practice book for advancing piano students, and as a practical resource guide for teachers. It is divided into eleven parts. Parts 1–3 provide foundational tools relating to scale, chord and arpeggio playing, and include traditional fingerings and exercises for developing precision, speed, agility and clarity of tone. Parts 4–11 provide numerous exercises and etudes that focus on a variety of technical challenges including finger independence, evenness in tone between the hands, double notes, trills, repeated notes, rotation, hand alternation, and chromatic patterns.

The materials are presented with little or no text, as we believe subtleties in presentation are best left to the skills of the experienced teacher. Editorial suggestions have been added for fingering (including alternate fingering) and dynamics. Tempo and metronome markings are used only when specified by the composer. It is our hope that the wide variety of sources will provide ample opportunity for advancing pianists to develop technical command of the instrument.

Teachers will wish to tailor the presentation of fundamental technical skills (Parts 1–3) and the exercises and etudes (Parts 4–11) to the needs of the individual student. Generally, materials are presented sequentially within each section, moving from easier to more challenging technical demands. A balanced and varied technical regime may also be accomplished by freely combining materials from a number of sections concurrently.

Students a ___ ___ lynamics and articulations in each study (for example, *Suggested Variants of Hanon*, page 33), to enhance attentive listening and to develop tonal control. Initially, all studies should be practiced slowly, with careful attention to physical ease and comfort; tempos should then be increased gradually, to ensure evenness in tone quality and technical control. Those with small hands may need to alter fingering, delete notes or skip some exercises entirely. If there is any pain, discontinue playing the exercise.

We would like to thank the following libraries for their services, as their contributions provided us the opportunity to select from the many thousands of etudes and exercises necessary to compile a book of this nature: Bates College, Cameron University, Cleveland Public Library, Detroit Public Library, Eastman School of Music, Illinois Wesleyan University, Kansas State University, Pacific Lutheran University, Southern Baptist Theological Seminary, Tulane University, University of California at Berkeley, University of Nebraska at Kearney, University of Nevada at Las Vegas, University of Oregon at Eugene, University of Wisconsin at Eau Claire, and Vanderbilt University. We also wish to express our sincere appreciation to Morty and Iris Manus, E. L. Lancaster, Victoria McArthur and all the members of the editorial, artistic, technical and administrative staff at Alfred Music for their continued support and unfailing commitment to quality and excellence in their educational publications and artistic editions.

Valerie Cisler and Maurice Hinson

FUNDAMENTAL SKILLS

Part One 🎹 *Scales*

Part Two 🎹 *Chords*

Part Three 🎹 *Arpeggios*

EXERCISES AND ETUDES

Part One ❈ Scales

Preparation

1 Passing the Thumb Under

Aloys Schmitt (1788–1866)
from *Preparatory Exercises*, Op. 16, Section II, Nos. 1–11

2 Passing the Thumb Under

Franz Liszt (1811–1886)
from *Technical Exercises for the Piano*, Book II, No. 47

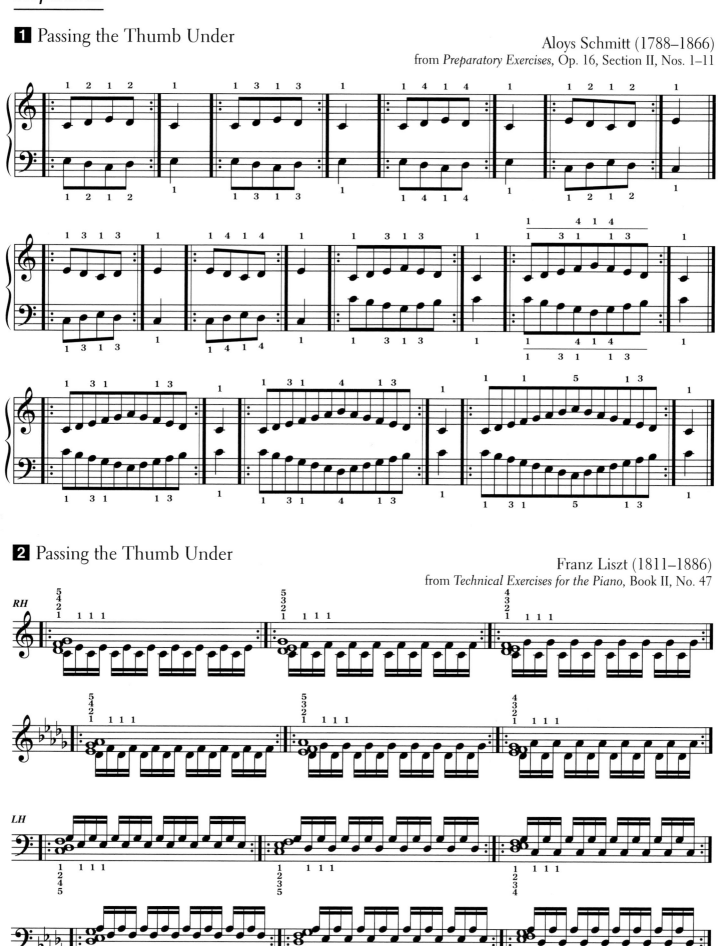

Major and Harmonic Minor Scale Fingerings

3 Group I Keys: C, G, D, A, E Major and Minor

   Ⓐ RH 4th finger on 7th degree

   Ⓑ LH 4th finger on 2nd degree

Traditional Scale Fingering Rules

▲ *The thumb does not play on black keys.*

▲ *The 4th finger is used only once in an octave.*

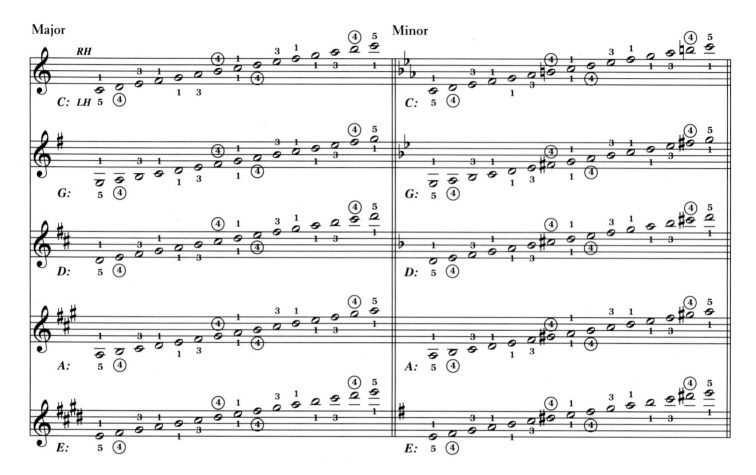

4 Group II Keys: B, F♯, C♯ Major and Minor

   Ⓐ RH 4th finger on A♯

   Ⓑ LH 4th finger on F♯

Exceptions: F♯ minor RH 4th finger on G♯

                      C♯ minor RH 4th finger on D♯

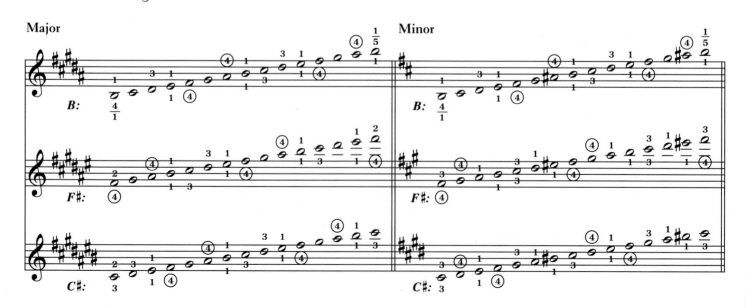

5 Group III Keys: A♭ Major & G♯ Minor; E♭, B♭ and F Major and Minor

    Ⓐ RH 4th finger on A♯/B♭   **Exception:** LH F major and minor 4th finger on G

    Ⓑ LH 4th finger on 4th degree

Major   Minor

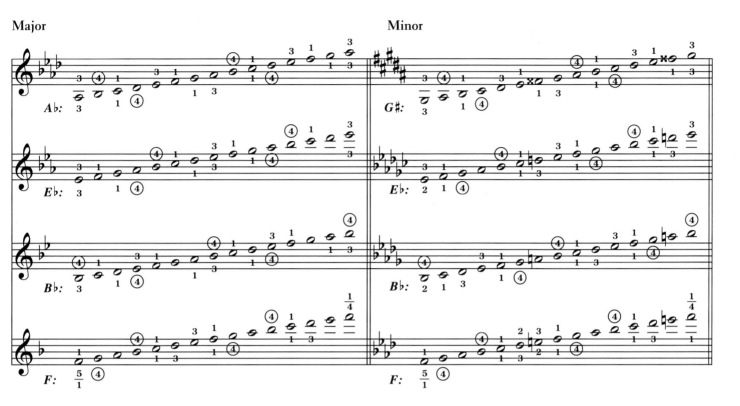

Lateral Shifts

6 Blocking Groups of Twos (2-3) and Threes (2-3-4) on Selected Scales

C Major

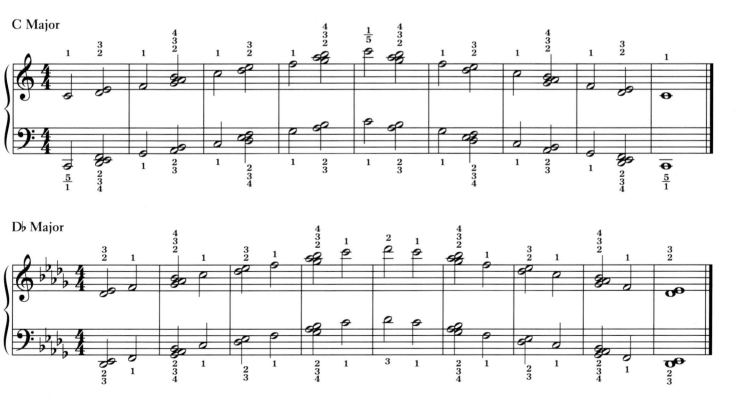

D♭ Major

Block all major and minor scales in a similar manner.

7 With the Thumb

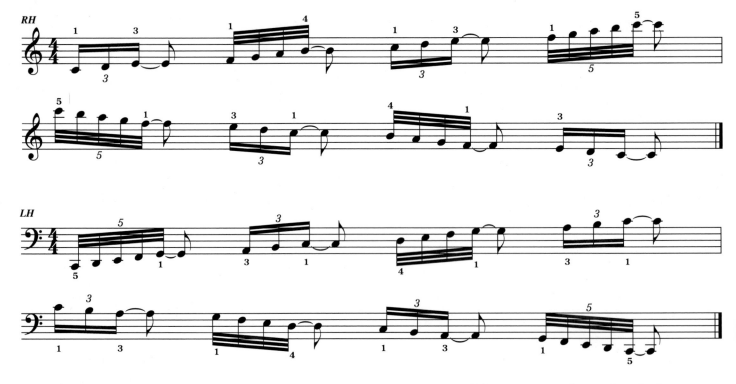

Transpose to all keys. Use traditional scale fingerings.

Accelerating Scales

Practice Suggestions for **8**

Ⓐ Practice all major and minor scales ♩ = 56–160.

Ⓑ Listen carefully for evenness on tone.

Ⓒ Use a variety of touches and articulations:

▲ legato   ▲ staccato   ▲ leggiero

Ⓓ Use a variety of dynamics:

▲ one dynamic level throughout

▲ **pp** to **ff**   ▲ $\leq$ $\geq$ ▲ $\geq$ $\leq$ ▲ one hand **p** and the other **f**

▲ one hand $\leq$ $\geq$ while the other $\geq$ $\leq$

Ⓔ Use a variety of rhythms:

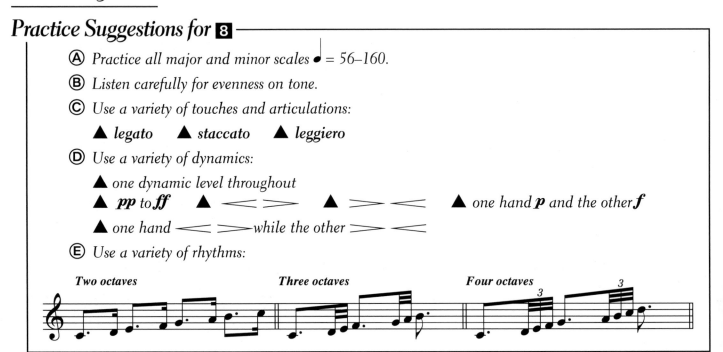

8 Quarters, Eighths, Triplets and Sixteenths

Play LH one octave below RH.

Quarters

Eighths

Triplets

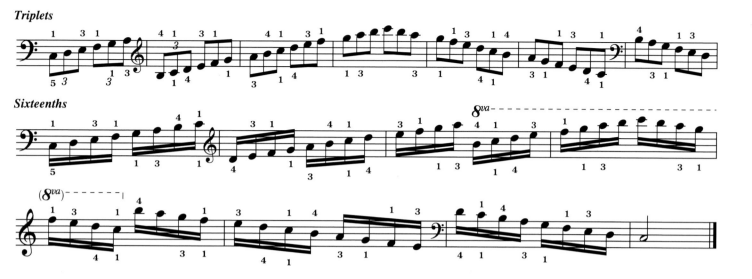

Sixteenths

9 Using "Add-On" Technique

Play LH one octave below RH.

Continue pattern downward.

Transpose to all keys.

10 Using "Add-On" Technique

Play LH one octave below RH.

Transpose to all keys.

11 Five-Note Groupings in Four Octaves

Play LH one octave below RH.

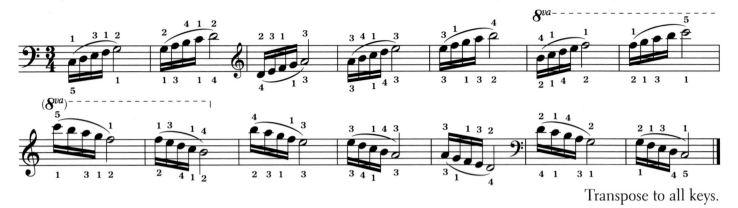

Transpose to all keys.

12 Nine-Note Groupings in Four Octaves

Play LH one octave below RH.

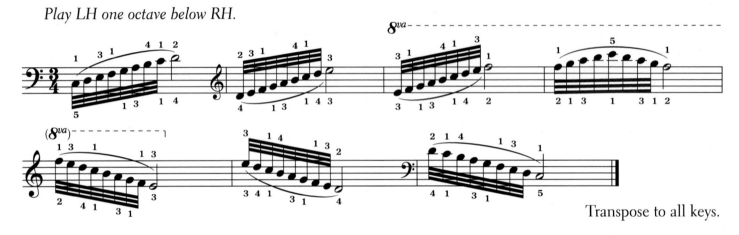

Transpose to all keys.

Rhythmic Variants—Contrasting Note Values Between the Hands

13 Four against Two   **14** Three against Two   **15** Two against Three

16 Four against Three   **17** Three against Four

18 The Grand Scale Form

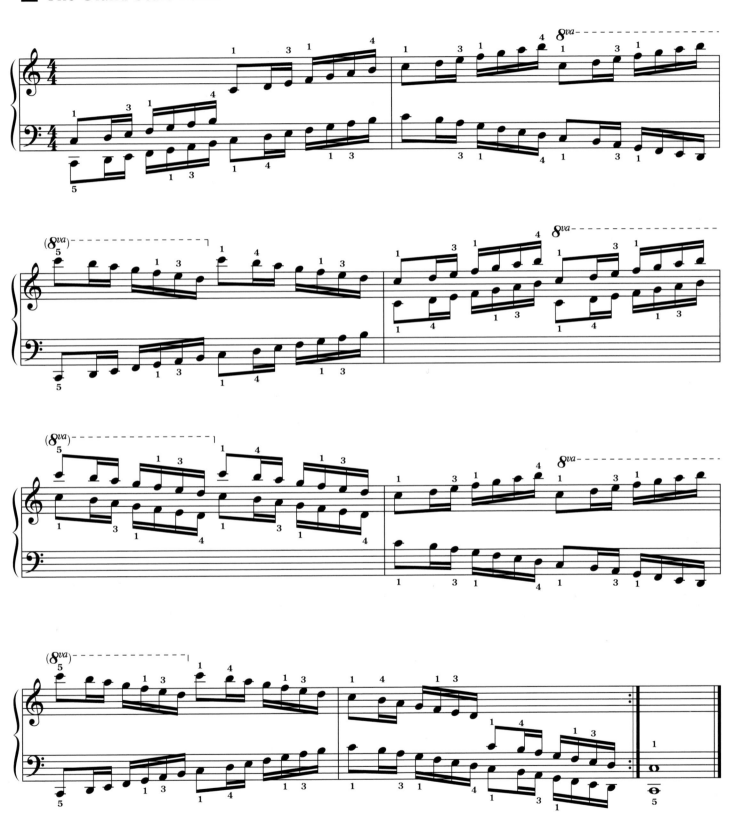

Transpose to all keys.

19 Major Scale in Thirds

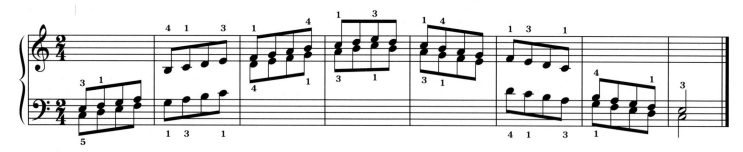

Transpose to all keys.

20 Harmonic Minor Scale in Thirds

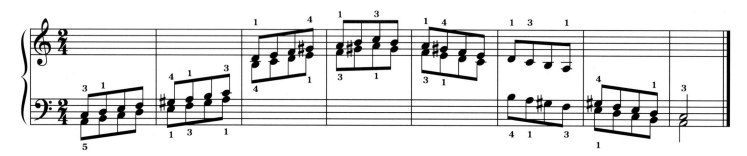

Transpose to all keys.

21 Major Scale in Sixths

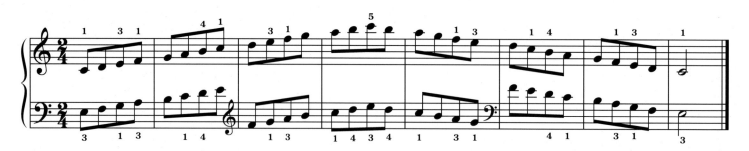

Transpose to all keys.

22 Harmonic Minor Scale in Sixths

Transpose to all keys.

23 Major Scale in Tenths

Transpose to all keys.

24 Harmonic Minor Scale in Tenths

Transpose to all keys.

25 Traditional Legato Fingering

When playing more than one octave, use the fingering in parentheses.

Aloys Schmitt (1788–1866)
from *Preparatory Exercises*, Op. 16
Section III, "Scales in Double Thirds"

C major
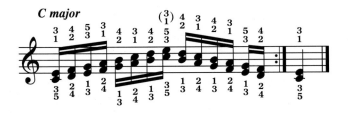

A minor

G major

E minor
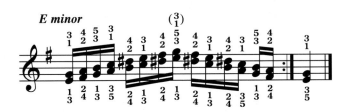

D major
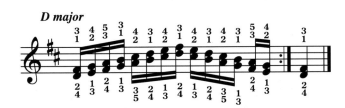

B minor

A major

F♯ minor

E major
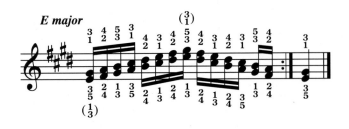

C♯ minor
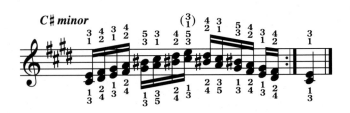

B major

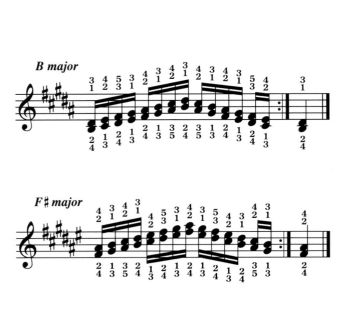

G# minor

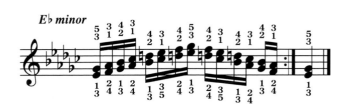

F# major

Eb minor

Db major

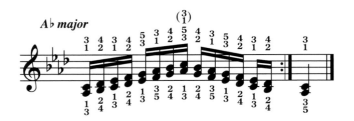

Bb minor

Ab major

F minor

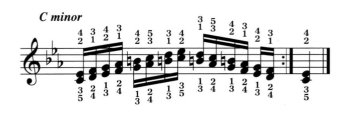

Eb major

C minor

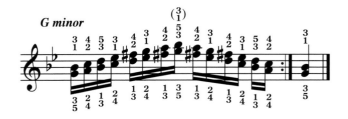

Bb major

G minor

F major

D minor

Chromatic—Parallel Motion

26 Single Notes

Practice all three fingering options.

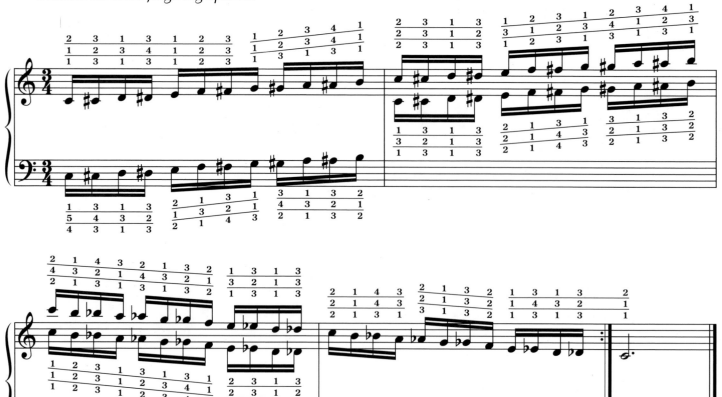

27 Major Thirds

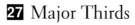

28 Minor Thirds

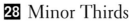

29 Major Sixths

30 Minor Sixths

31 Major Tenths

32 Minor Tenths

Chromatic—Contrary Motion

33 Starting on D (with Matching Fingering)

Part Two ❧ *Chords*

Triads

1 Major, Augmented, Minor, Diminished

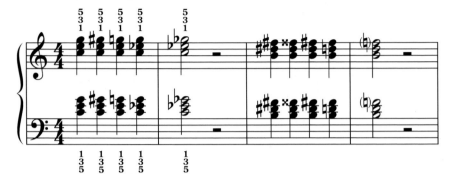

Continue downward by half steps until…

2 Inversions (Major, Minor, Diminished)

Continue pattern upward through all keys.

3 Inversions (Broken Chords)

Play LH one or two octaves below RH.

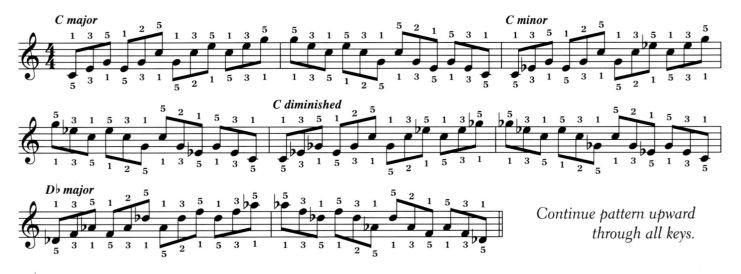

Continue pattern upward through all keys.

4 Inversions (Extended Four-Note Broken Chords)

Play LH one or two octaves below RH.

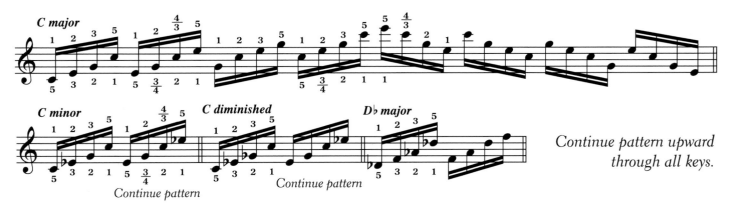

Continue pattern upward through all keys.

Continue pattern

Continue pattern

5 Inversions (Extended Broken $\frac{6}{4}$ Chords)

Play LH one or two octaves below RH.

Continue pattern upward through all keys.

6 Extended Broken-Chord Pattern

Play LH one or two octaves below RH.

C major

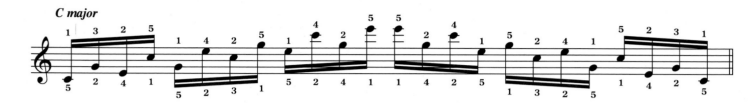

C minor   **C diminished**   **Db major**

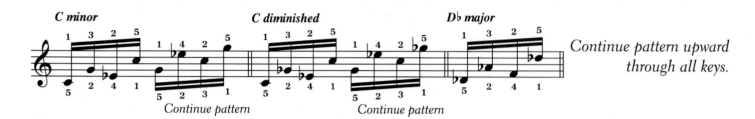

Continue pattern upward through all keys.

Continue pattern   *Continue pattern*

Seventh Chords

7 Five Types of Blocked Seventh Chords in Root Position

Major	Dominant	Minor	Half Diminished	Fully Diminished
Cmaj7	C7	Cm7	Cm7(b5)	C°7
Major triad with Major seventh	Major triad with Minor seventh	Minor triad with Minor seventh	Diminished triad with Minor seventh	Diminished triad with Diminished seventh

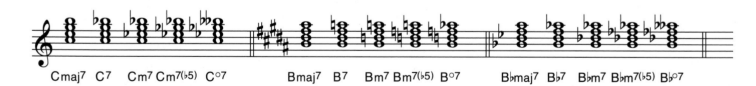

Cmaj7 C7   Cm7 Cm7(b5) C°7   Bmaj7   B7   Bm7 Bm7(b5) B°7   Bbmaj7 Bb7   Bbm7 Bbm7(b5) Bb°7

Continue pattern downward through all keys.

8 Inversions (Broken and Blocked)

Play LH one or two octaves below RH.

Continue pattern upward through all keys.

Part Three ❀ Arpeggios

Triads (Fingering Patterns)

1 Group I Keys: C, F, G Major

Key		Fingering	
C	RH:	1 2 3	1 2 3 5
	LH:	5 4 2	1 4 2 1
F	RH:	1 2 3	1 2 3 5
	LH:	5 4 2	1 4 2 1
G	RH:	1 2 3	1 2 3 5
	LH:	5 4 2	1 4 2 1

2 Group I Keys:
C, D, D♯/E♭, E, F, G, A, B Minor

Key		Fingering	
C	RH:	1 2̇ 3 *	1 2̇ 3 5
	LH:	5 4̇ 2	1 4̇ 2 1
D	RH:	1 2 3	1 2 3 5
	LH:	5 4 2	1 4 2 1
D♯/E♭	RH:	1̇ 2̇ 3̇	1̇ 2̇ 3̇ 5̇
	LH:	5̇ 4̇ 2̇	1̇ 4̇ 2̇ 1̇
E	RH:	1 2 3	1 2 3 5
	LH:	5 4 2	1 4 2 1
F	RH:	1 2̇ 3	1 2̇ 3 5
	LH:	5 4̇ 2	1 4̇ 2 1
G	RH:	1 2̇ 3	1 2̇ 3 5
	LH:	5 4̇ 2	1 4̇ 2 1
A	RH:	1 2 3	1 2 3 5
	LH:	5 4 2	1 4 2 1
B	RH:	1 2 3̇	1 2 3̇ 5
	LH:	5 4 2̇	1 4 2̇ 1

---

3 Group II Keys: D, A, E, B, F♯/G♭ Major

Key		Fingering	
D	RH:	1 2̇ 3	1 2̇ 3 5
	LH:	5 3̇ 2	1 3̇ 2 1
A	RH:	1 2̇ 3	1 2̇ 3 5
	LH:	5 3̇ 2	1 3̇ 2 1
E	RH:	1 2̇ 3	1 2̇ 3 5
	LH:	5 3̇ 2	1 3̇ 2 1
B	RH:	1 2̇ 3̇	1 2̇ 3 5
	LH:	5 3̇ 2̇	1 3̇ 2 1
F♯/G♭	RH:	1̇ 2̇ 3̇	1̇ 2̇ 3̇ 5̇
	LH:	5̇ 3̇ 2̇	1̇ 3̇ 2̇ 1̇

*A dot (•) above a finger number indicates a black key.

4 Group III Keys: C♯/D♭, E♭, A♭ Major

All Black-White-Black Patterns

E♭ major

Key	Fingering						
C♯/D♭	RH:	4 1 2	4 1 2 4
	LH:	2 1 4	2 1 4 2
E♭	RH:	4 1 2	4 1 2 4
	LH:	2 1 4	2 1 4 2
A♭	RH:	4 1 2	4 1 2 4
	LH:	2 1 4	2 1 4 2

5 Group III Keys: C♯/D♭, F♯, G♯/A♭ Minor

All Black-White-Black Patterns

Key	Fingering						
C♯/D♭	RH:	4 1 2	4 1 2 4
	LH:	2 1 4	2 1 4 2
F♯	RH:	4 1 2	4 1 2 4
	LH:	2 1 4	2 1 4 2
G♯/A♭	RH:	4 1 2	4 1 2 4
	LH:	2 1 4	2 1 4 2

6 Group IV Key: B♭ Major

B♭ major

Key	Fingering						
B♭	RH:	4 1 2	4 1 2 4
	LH:	3 2 1	3 2 1 3

7 Group IV Key: B♭ Minor

B♭ minor

Key	Fingering						
A♯/B♭	RH:	2 3 1	2 3 1 2
	LH:	3 2 1	3 2 1 3

Triads (Root Position and Inversions)

8 Four Types of Triads in Triplet Rhythm (Augmented, Major, Minor, Diminished)

Play LH one or two octaves below RH.

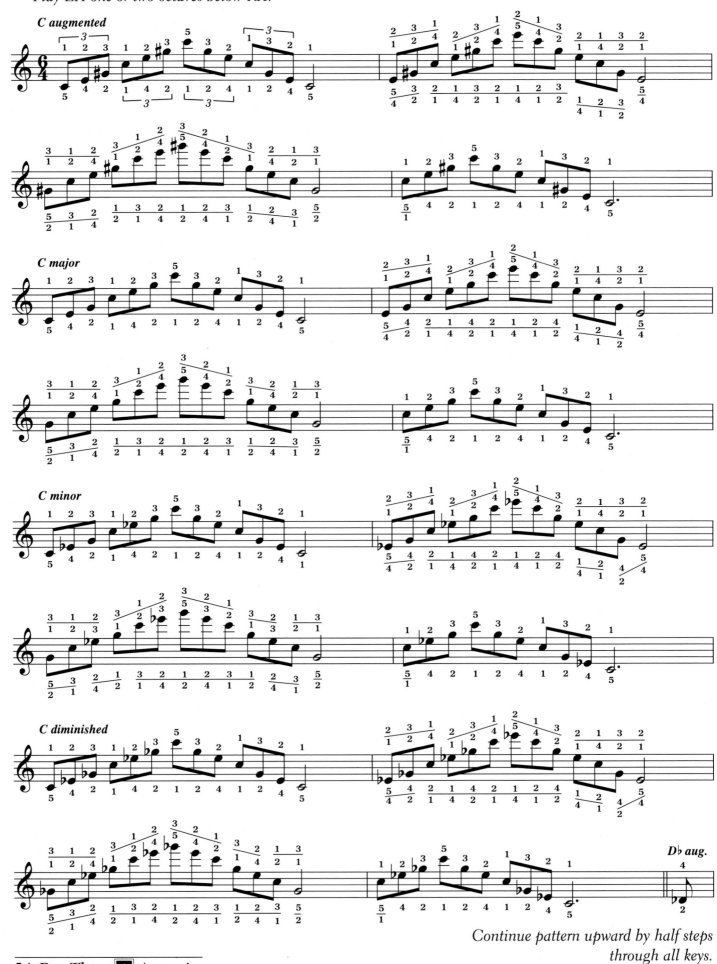

Continue pattern upward by half steps through all keys.

Seventh Chords

9 Five Types of Broken Seventh Chords in Root Position
(Major, Dominant, Minor, Half Diminished, Fully Diminished)

Play LH one or two octaves below RH.

Major
Cmaj7

Dominant
C7

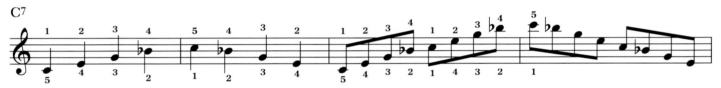

Minor
Cm7

Half Diminished
Cm7(♭5)

Fully Diminished
C°7

*Continue pattern upward
through all keys.*

Dominant Seventh Chords (Fingering Patterns)

10 Group I Keys: C⁷, F⁷, G⁷, D⁷, A⁷, E⁷, B⁷/C♭⁷

C⁷	RH:	1 2 3 4•*	1 2 3 4 5
	LH:	5 4 3 2	1 4 3 2 1
F⁷	RH:	1 2 3 4	1 2 3 4 5
	LH:	5 4 3 2	1 4 3 2 1
G⁷	RH:	1 2 3 4	1 2 3 4 5
	LH:	5 4 3 2	1 4 3 2 1
D⁷	RH:	1 2 3 4	1 2 3 4 5
	LH:	5 4 3 2	1 4 3 2 1

A⁷	RH:	1 2 3 4	1 2 3 4 5
	LH:	5 4 3 2	1 4 3 2 1
E⁷	RH:	1 2 3 4	1 2 3 4 5
	LH:	5 4 3 2	1 4 3 2 1
B⁷/C♭⁷	RH:	1 2 3 4	1 2 3 4 5
	LH:	5 4 3 2	1 4 3 2 1

11 Group II Keys: C♯⁷/D♭⁷, A♭⁷, E♭⁷

C♯⁷/D♭⁷	RH:	4 1 2 3	4 1 2 3 4
	LH:	2 1 4 3	2 1 4 3 2
A♭⁷	RH:	4 1 2 3	4 1 2 3 4
	LH:	2 1 4 3	2 1 4 3 2

E♭⁷	RH:	4 1 2 3	4 1 2 3 4
	LH:	2 1 4 3	2 1 4 3 2

12 Group III Keys: F♯⁷/G♭⁷, B♭⁷

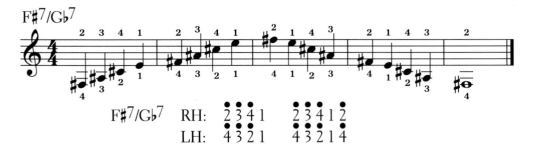

F♯⁷/G♭⁷	RH:	2 3 4 1	2 3 4 1 2
	LH:	4 3 2 1	4 3 2 1 4

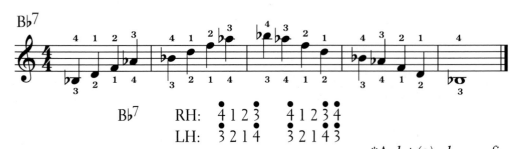

B♭⁷	RH:	4 1 2 3	4 1 2 3 4
	LH:	3 2 1 4	3 2 1 4 3

*A dot (•) above a finger number indicates a black key.

Dominant Seventh Arpeggios (Root Position and Inversions)

13 Two Octaves Ascending and Descending

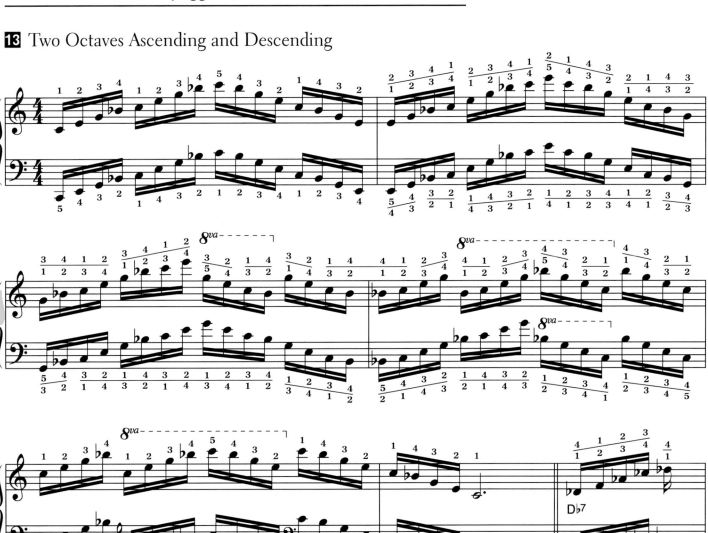

*Continue pattern upward
through all keys.*

14 Grand Style

Transpose to all keys.

Diminished Seventh Chords* (Fingering Patterns)

15 Group I Keys: C°7, G°7, D°7

C°7

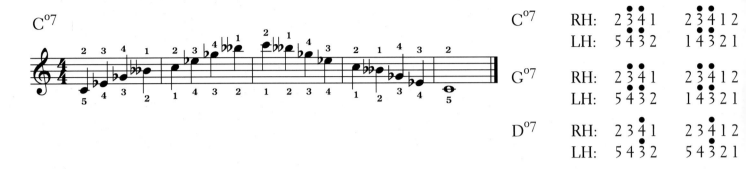

C°7	RH:	2 3 4 1	2 3 4 1 2
	LH:	5 4 3 2	1 4 3 2 1
G°7	RH:	2 3 4 1	2 3 4 1 2
	LH:	5 4 3 2	1 4 3 2 1
D°7	RH:	2 3 4 1	2 3 4 1 2
	LH:	5 4 3 2	5 4 3 2 1

16 Group II Keys: A°7, E°7, B°7/C♭°7

A°7

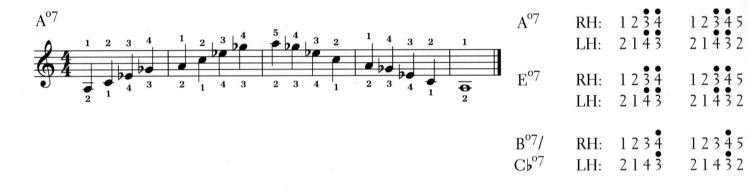

A°7	RH:	1 2 3 4	1 2 3 4 5
	LH:	2 1 4 3	2 1 4 3 2
E°7	RH:	1 2 3 4	1 2 3 4 5
	LH:	2 1 4 3	2 1 4 3 2
B°7/ C♭°7	RH:	1 2 3 4	1 2 3 4 5
	LH:	2 1 4 3	2 1 4 3 2

17 Group III Keys: F♯°7/G♭°7, C♯°7/D♭°7, G♯°7/A♭°7

F♯°7/G♭°7

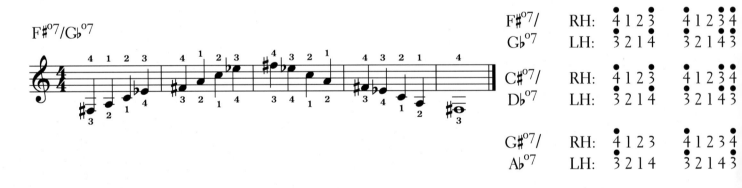

F♯°7/ G♭°7	RH:	4 1 2 3	4 1 2 3 4
	LH:	3 2 1 4	3 2 1 4 3
C♯°7/ D♭°7	RH:	4 1 2 3	4 1 2 3 4
	LH:	3 2 1 4	3 2 1 4 3
G♯°7/ A♭°7	RH:	4 1 2 3	4 1 2 3 4
	LH:	3 2 1 4	3 2 1 4 3

18 Group IV Keys: E♭°7, B♭°7, F°7

E♭°7

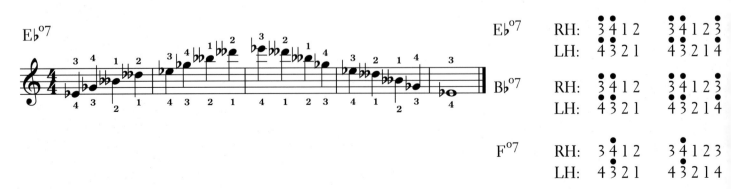

E♭°7	RH:	3 4 1 2	3 4 1 2 3
	LH:	4 3 2 1	4 3 2 1 4
B♭°7	RH:	3 4 1 2	3 4 1 2 3
	LH:	4 3 2 1	4 3 2 1 4
F°7	RH:	3 4 1 2	3 4 1 2 3
	LH:	4 3 2 1	4 3 2 1 4

*All diminished seventh chords are derived from either C, C♯/D♭ or D.

Diminished Seventh Arpeggios (Root Position and Inversions)

19 Two Octaves Ascending and Descending

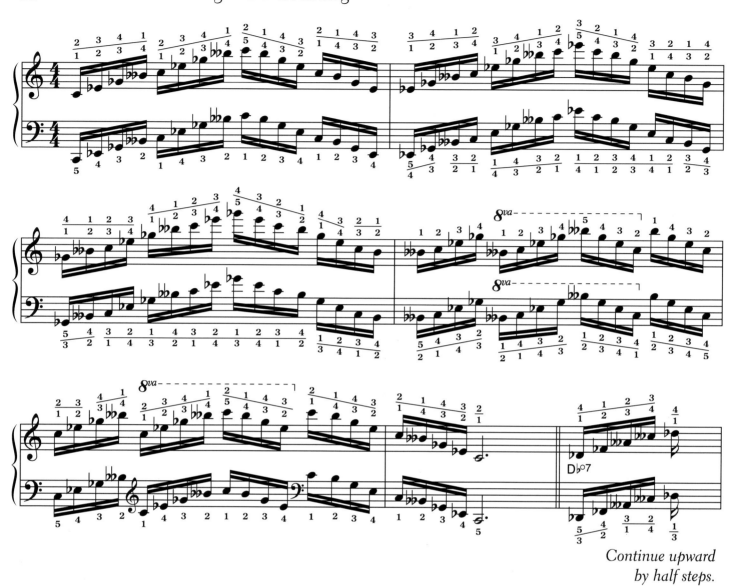

Continue upward by half steps.

20 Grand Style

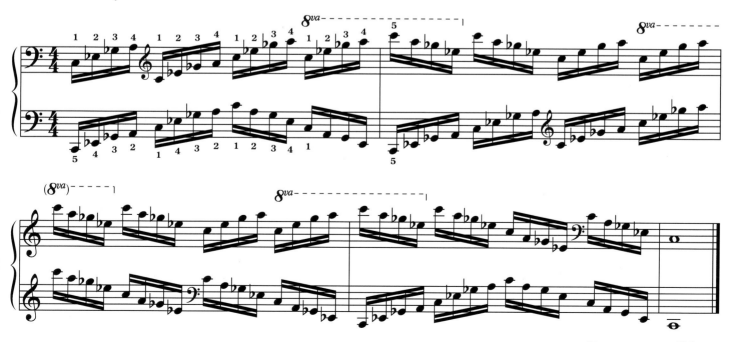

Transpose to all keys.

Seventh Chord Arpeggio Studies

21 Four-Octave Patterns

Play each four-octave arpeggio pattern (1, 2 and 3) with all four sets of
fingering (a, b, c and d). Play hands separate and together with one
octave between the hands. Transpose to all keys.

attr. to Sergei Rachmaninoff
(1873–1943)

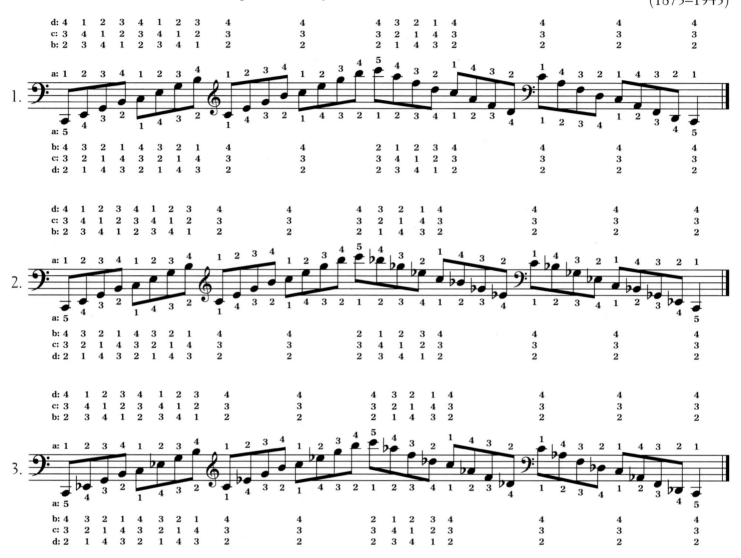

Note: Students may find it easier to perform the above patterns by viewing them in block form.
For example:

Beginning on C:

(1)   *(2)*   *(3)*

Beginning on D:

(1)   *(2)*   *(3)*

Beginning on Db:

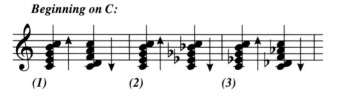

(1)   *(2)*   *(3)*

Beginning on Eb:

(1)   *(2)*   *(3)*

Transpose to all keys.

Fingering for above arpeggios:

	a:	b:	c:	d:
RH	1 2 3 4 (5)	2 3 4 1 (2)	3 4 1 2 (3)	4 1 2 3 (4)
LH	5 4 3 2 (1)	4 3 2 1 (2)	3 2 1 4 (3)	2 1 4 3 (2)

22 Minor Thirds Added Above (Thumb Passes Under)*

Play each group four times.

Frédéric Chopin
(1810–1849)

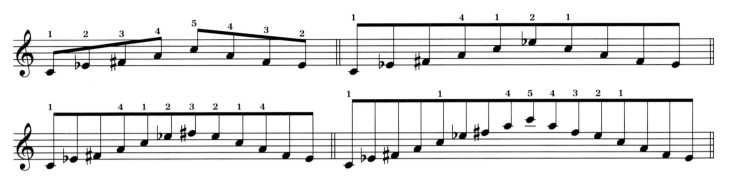

23 Minor Thirds Added Below

Play each group four times.

24 Minor Thirds Added Above and Below

Play each group four times.

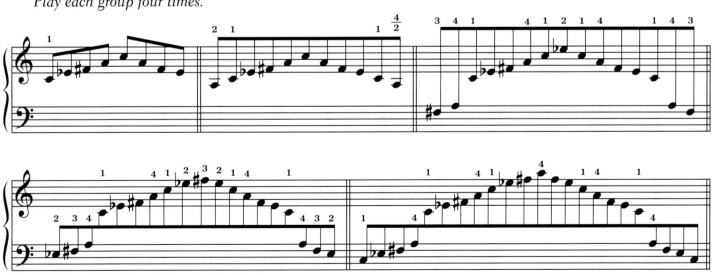

*Note: Chopin provides only the RH fingerings for these studies, as cited in **Chopin's Teaching and His Students**, by Jeanne Holland, Appendix C: "Chopin's Exercises for His Niece Louise," Ph.D. Dissertation, 1973.

Part Four 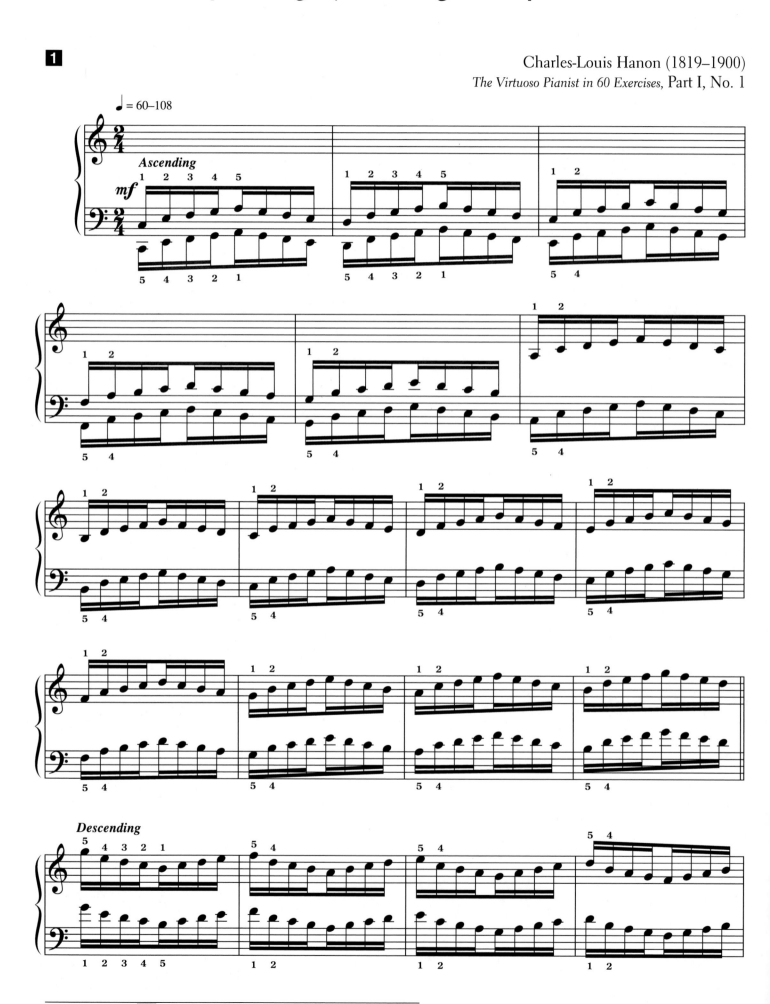 *Speed, Agility and Finger Independence*

1

Charles-Louis Hanon (1819–1900)
The Virtuoso Pianist in 60 Exercises, Part I, No. 1

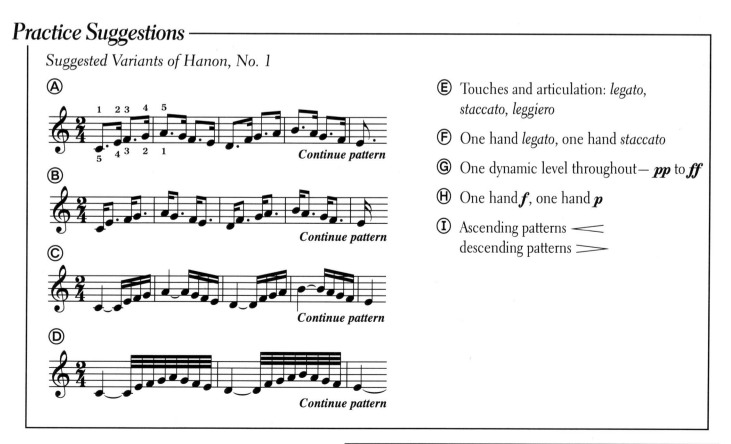

Practice Suggestions

Suggested Variants of Hanon, No. 1

A

Continue pattern

B

Continue pattern

C

Continue pattern

D

Continue pattern

E Touches and articulation: *legato, staccato, leggiero*

F One hand *legato*, one hand *staccato*

G One dynamic level throughout— *pp* to *ff*

H One hand *f*, one hand *p*

I Ascending patterns ⟨
descending patterns ⟩

2 Five-Finger Patterns with Sustained Notes

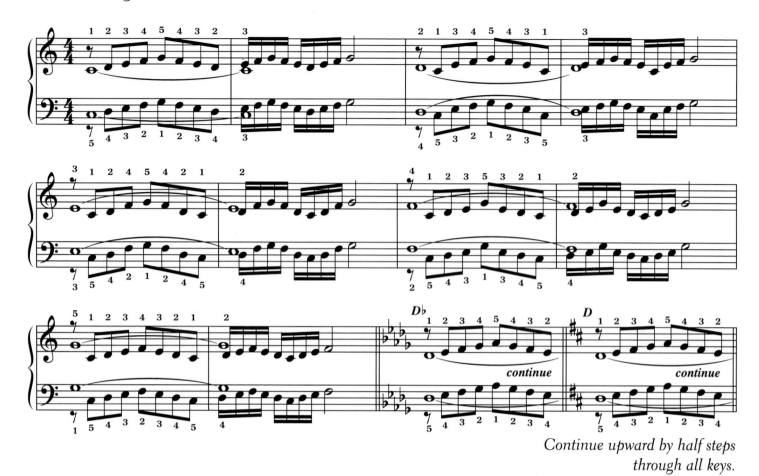

Continue upward by half steps
through all keys.

3 Five-Finger Patterns with Sustained Notes

Continue upward by half steps
through all keys.

Ascending and Descending Patterns with Sustained Notes

Isidor Philipp (1863–1958)
from *Complete School of Technic for the Piano*
"Exercises in Velocity," Nos. 18–21

4 *Play LH one or two octaves below RH.*

5 *Play LH one or two octaves below RH.*

6 *Play LH one or two octaves below RH.*

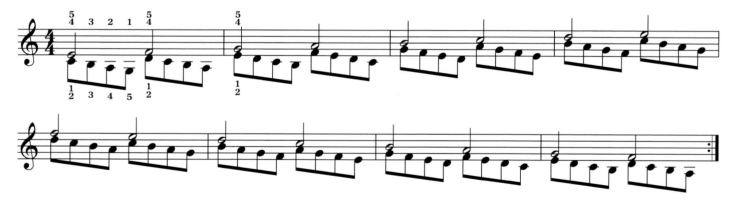

7 *Play LH one or two octaves below RH.*

8 Flexibilty and Independence of the Fingers

Isidor Philipp (1863–1958)
from *Complete School of Technic for the Piano*, No. 12

Continue upward by half steps
through all keys.

Finger Repetitions with Sustained Notes

Aloys Schmitt (1788–1866)
from *Preparatory Exercises*, Op. 16, Section I, Nos. 111–118

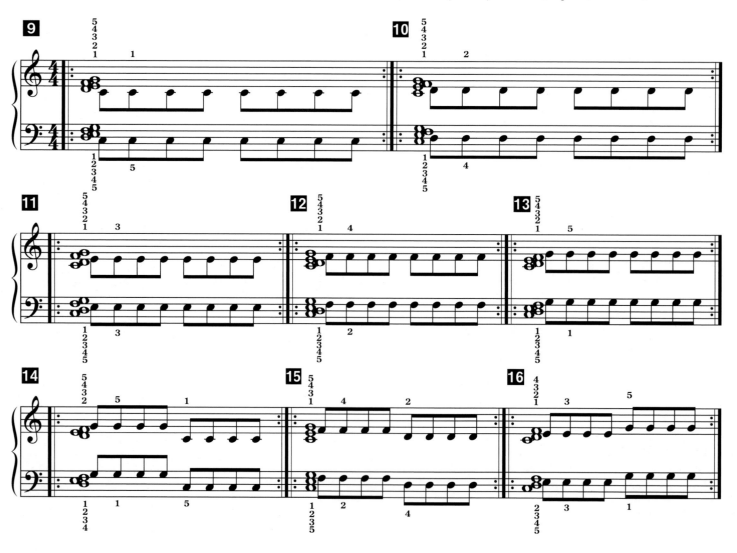

17 Three-Note Patterns with Sustained Double Thirds

Johann Pischna (1826–1890)
from *Technical Studies: 60 Progressive Exercises*, No. 7

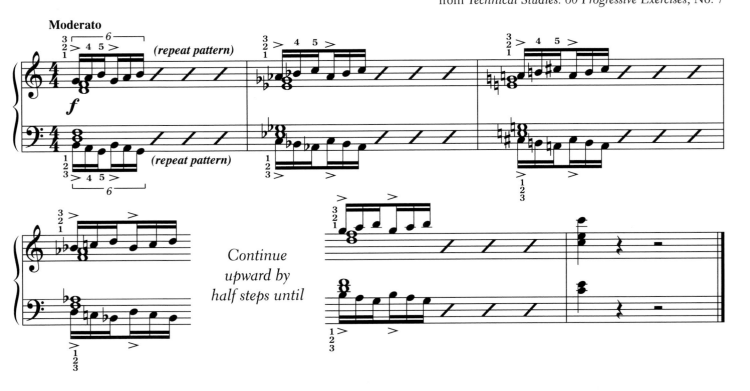

18 Passing the Thumb Under with Sustained Notes

Johann Pischna (1826–1890)
from *Technical Studies: 60 Progressive Exercises*, No. 14

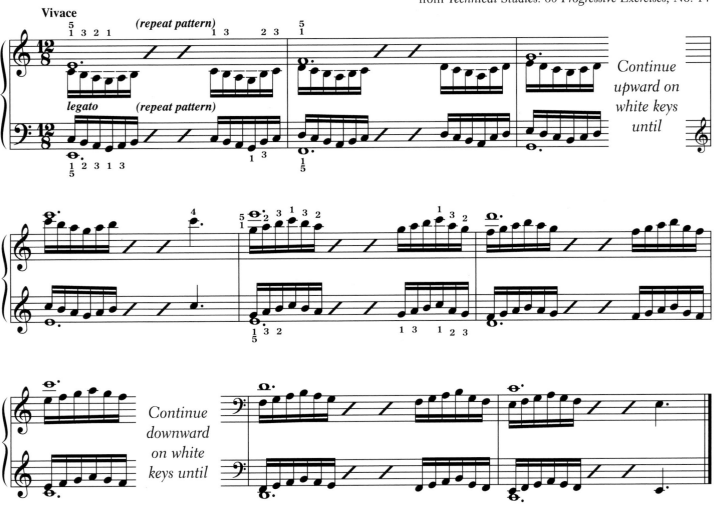

Johannes Brahms (1833–1897)
from *51 Exercises*, No. 24a

sempre ben legato

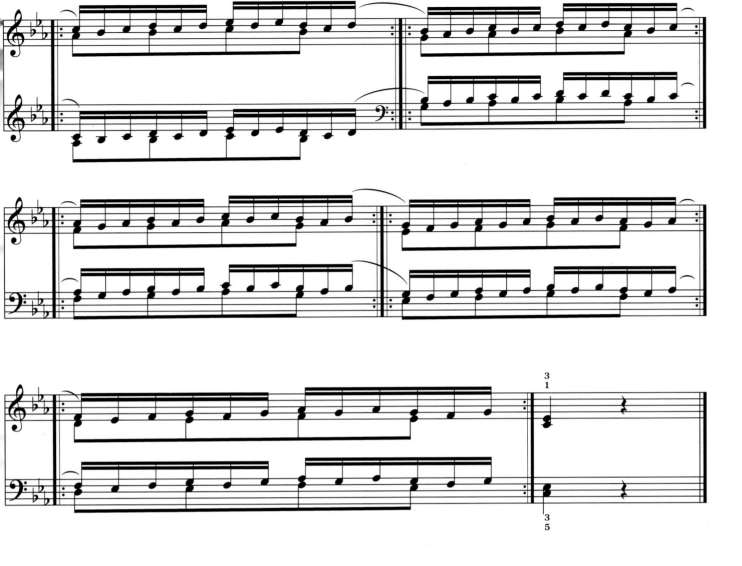

20 Broken Dominant Seventh Chord with Sustained Notes

Play LH two octaves below RH.

Transpose to all keys.

21 Broken Diminished Seventh Chord with Sustained Notes

Play LH two octaves below RH.

Transpose to all keys.

22 Etude in E Minor

Johann Baptist Cramer (1771–1858)
from *50 Selected Studies*, No. 2
(No. 20 from original 84 studies)

Cramer wrote the following footnote in the score: "This piece requires a firm touch in the outer fingers.
The middle fingers in both hands should move with ease to give the inner voices a natural melodic flow,
with a slight crescendo ascending and a slight decrescendo descending."

40 Part Four 🎹 *Speed, Agility and Finger Independence*

Moritz Moszkowski (1854–1925)
from 20 *Petite Etudes*, Op. 91, No. 4

Polyphonic Techniques

24 Opposing Rhythms in Two Parts—One Note Against Two

Alfred Cortot (1877–1962)
from *Rational Principles of the Pianoforte Technique*
Chapter III, Series C, "Polyphonic Technique," No. 3a (mm. 1, 2, 4)

25 Opposing Rhythms

Carl Czerny (1791–1857)
from *160 Eight-Measure Exercises*, Op. 821, No. 53

Part Five  *Even Tone Between the Hands*

1 Scale Passages Shared by Both Hands

LH = stems down, RH = stems up

Transpose to all keys.

2 Broken Chords

Friedrich Wieck (1785–1873)
from *Pianoforte Studies, Section I, No. 20*

3 Triads and Dominant Seventh Chords in 24 Keys—Circle of Fourths

Friedrich Wieck (1785–1873)
from *Pianoforte Studies*, Section II

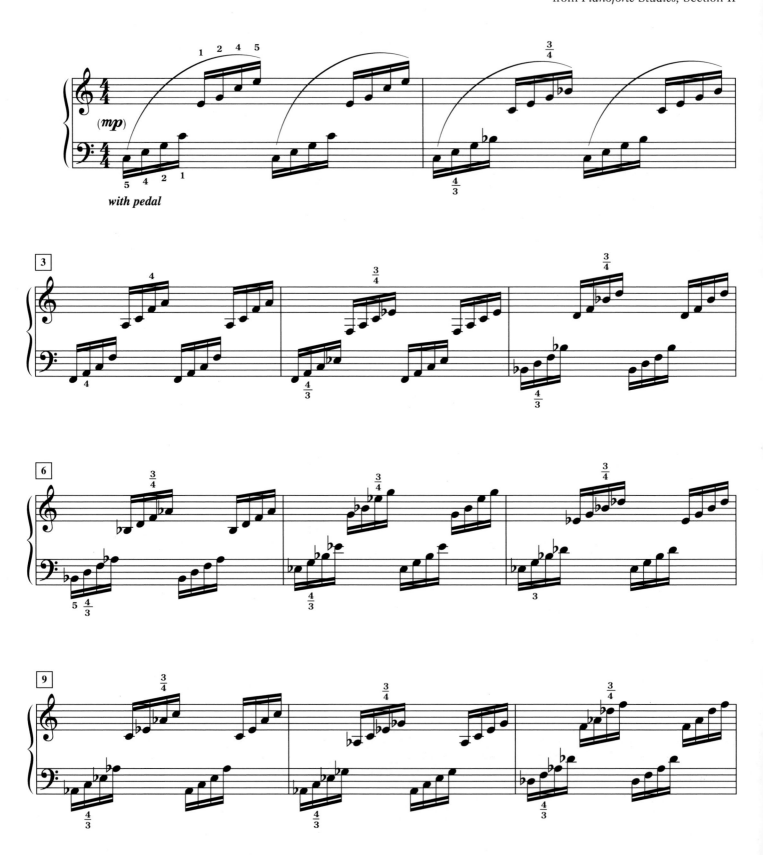

4 Study in C Major

Carl Czerny (1791–1857)
from Czerny-Germer *Selected Piano Studies,*
Op. 849, No. 29, Part II, No. 4

Part Six ❀ Double Notes

Double Thirds

Practice Suggestion

▲ Practice all double-note exercises and etudes with firm fingers and a supple wrist.

1 Thirds Parallel Motion

Continue upward by half steps through one octave.

2 Thirds Contrary Motion

Emphasis on outer hand

Continue upward by half steps through one octave.

3 Thirds Ascending and Descending

Play the two notes of each third exactly together and connect each group.

Friedrich Wieck (1785–1873)
from *Pianoforte Studies*, Section I, No. 20

Continue upward on white keys.

4 Detached Thirds

Play LH one or two octaves below RH.
Use fingering 3-1, 4-2, 3-5.

5 Broken Thirds

Ferruccio Busoni (1866–1924)
from *Exercises and Studies for the Piano*, Part I,
"Double Notes," No. 6

For RH only.

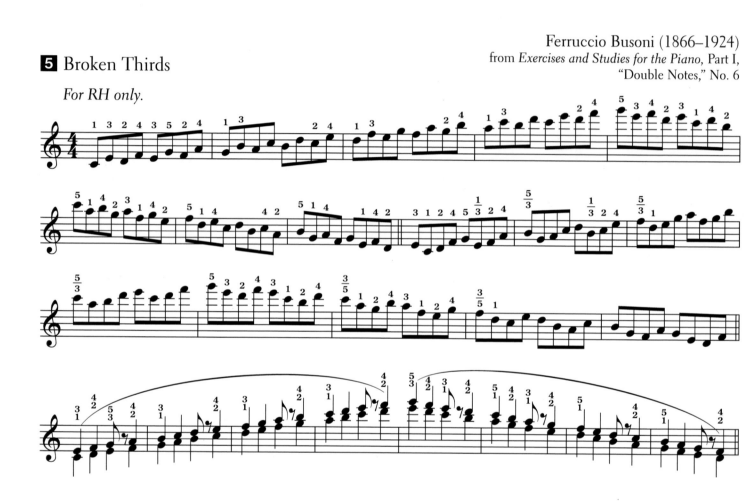

6 Legato Double-Third Scale in Contrary Motion

Ferruccio Busoni (1866–1924)
from *Exercises and Studies for the Piano*, Part I,
"Double Notes," No. 7

Moderato

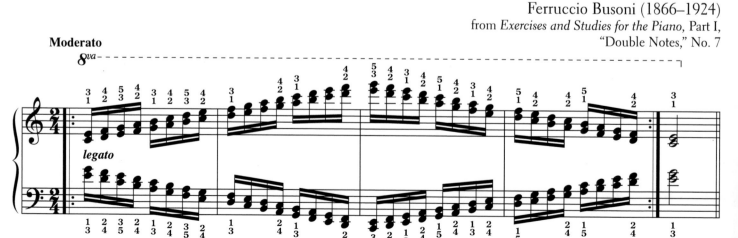

7 Thirds Crossing Hands

Friedrich Wieck (1785–1873)
from *Pianoforte Studies*, Section I, No. 11

Cross the hands quickly.

8 Etude in D Minor

Franz Liszt (1811–1886)
from *Etudes*, Op. 1, No. 4

9 Double Fourths

Isidor Philipp (1863–1958)
from *Complete School of Technic for the Piano*,
"Double Fourths," Nos. 2–5

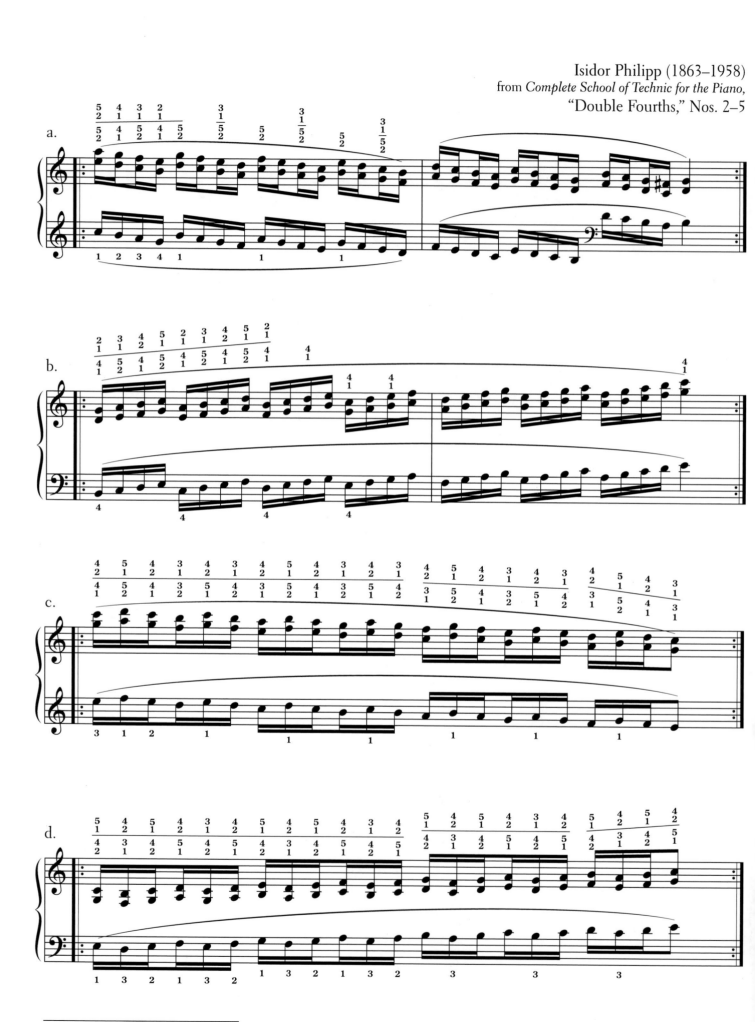

10 Thirds and Fourths—Leaps

Moritz Moszkowski (1854–1925)
from *School of Double Notes*, Op. 64, No. 18

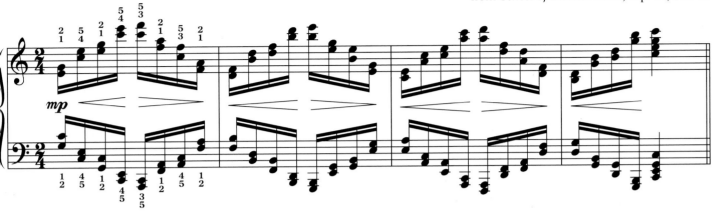

11 Detached Fifths

Play with one or two octaves between the hands.

12 Fourths and Fifths

Continue upward by half steps through all keys.

13 Fourths and Fifths

attr. to Sergei Rachmaninoff (1873–1943)

Continue upward by half steps through all keys.

14 Fourths

Béla Bartók (1881–1945)
from *Mikrokosmos*, Vol. V, No. 131

15 Broken Sixths

Play LH one or two octaves below RH.

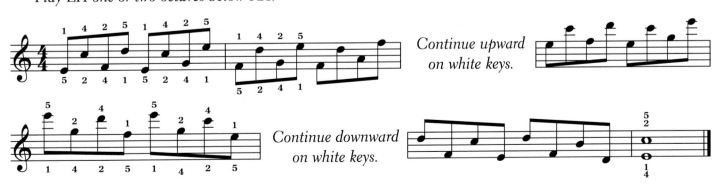

Continue upward on white keys.

Continue downward on white keys.

16 Legato Sixths

Play LH one or two octaves below RH.

Isidor Philipp (1863–1958)
from *Complete School of Technic for the Piano,*
Legato Double Sixths 3-4-5, No. 2

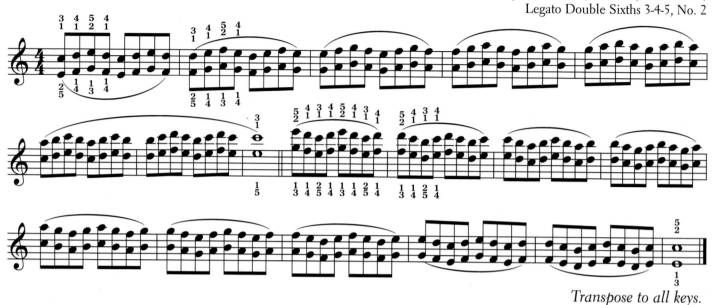

Transpose to all keys.

17 Legato Sixths

Play LH one or two octaves below RH.

Isidor Philipp (1863–1958)
from *Complete School of Technic for the Piano,*
Legato Double Sixths 2-3-4-5, No. 4

Transpose to all keys.

18 Detached Sixths

Play LH one or two octaves below RH.

19 Fifths and Sixths

Moritz Moszkowski (1854–1925)
from *School of Double Notes,* Op. 64, No. 5

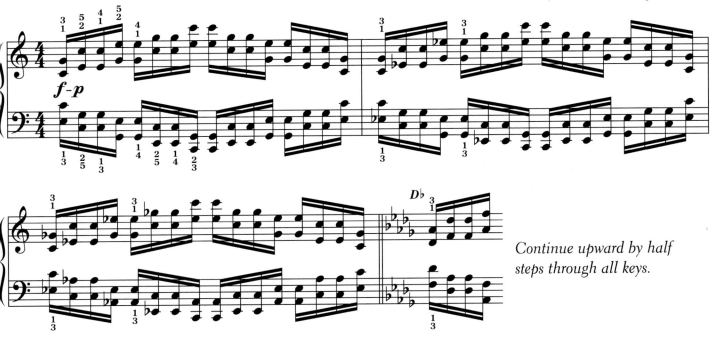

*Continue upward by half
steps through all keys.*

20 Detached Octaves

Play with one or two octaves between the hands.

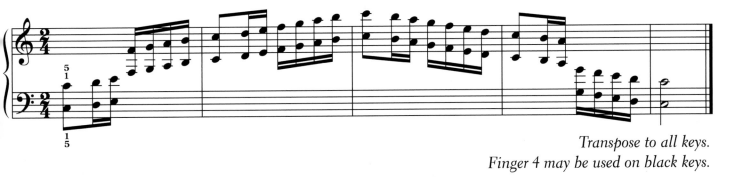

*Transpose to all keys.
Finger 4 may be used on black keys.*

21 Scale in Octaves—"Add-On" Exercise

Play with one octave between the hands.

*Continue upward by half
steps through all keys.*

22 Octaves from the Wrist

Isidor Philipp (1863–1958)
from *Complete School of Technic for the Piano*,
Octaves from the Wrist, No. 8

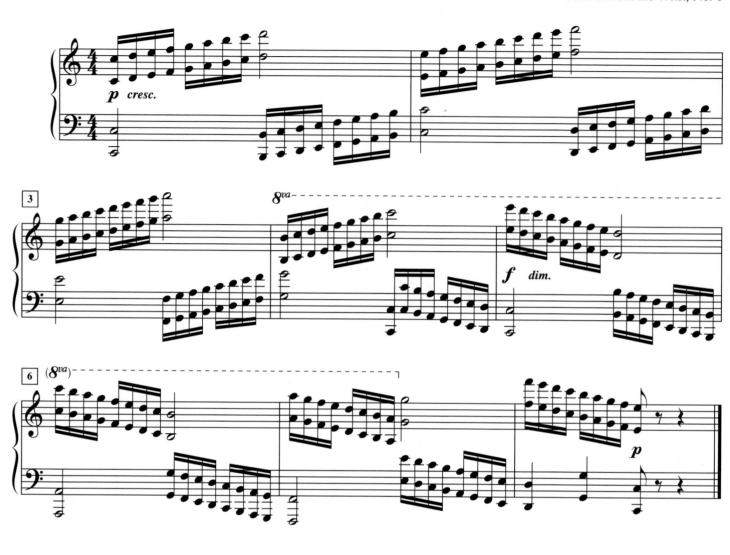

23 Scales in Octaves in the 24 Keys

Charles-Louis Hanon (1819–1900)
from *The Virtuoso Pianist in 60 Exercises*
Part 3, No. 53

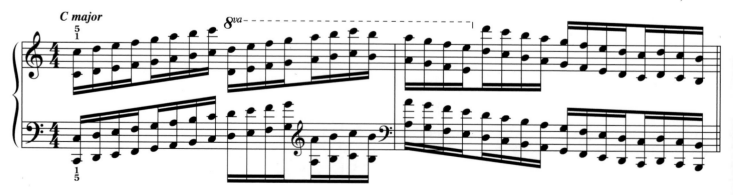

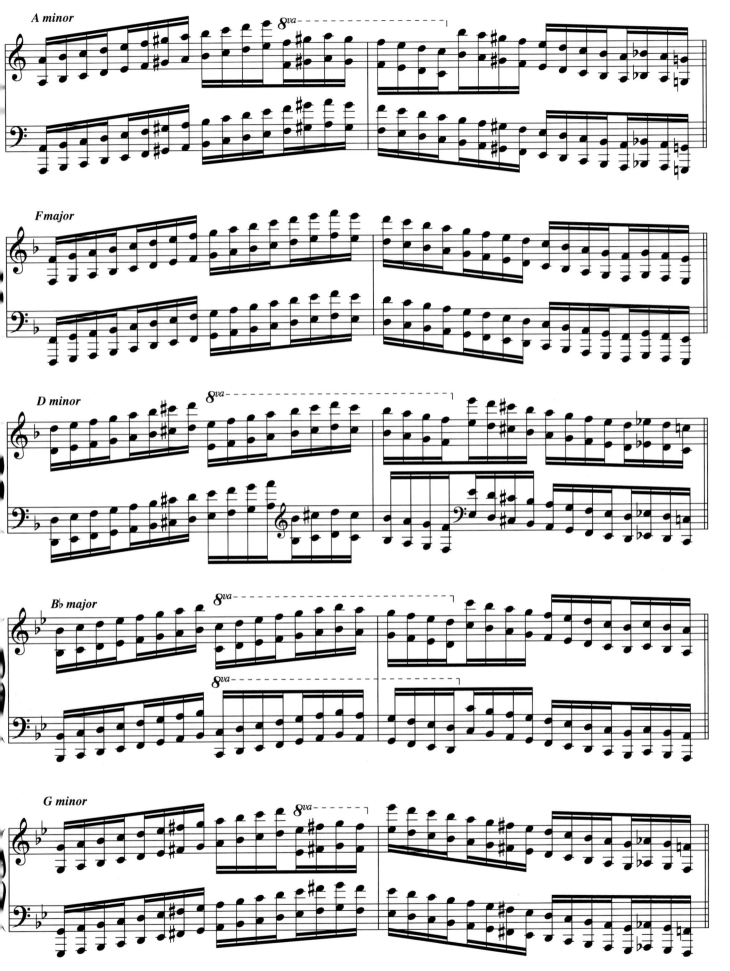

Continue through all major and minor keys.

24 Etude in C Major

Henri Bertini (1798–1876)
from *24 Etudes*, Op. 29, No. 22

25 Legato Octaves

Isidor Philipp (1863–1958)
from *Complete School of Technic for the Piano*
"Legato Octaves," Nos. 1–2

a.

b. *Play with one octave between the hands.*

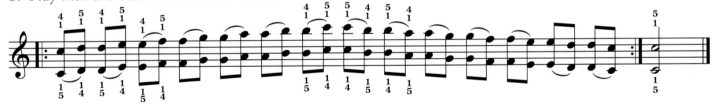

26 Broken Triads in Octaves (Augmented, Major, Minor, Diminished)

Play with one octave between the hands.

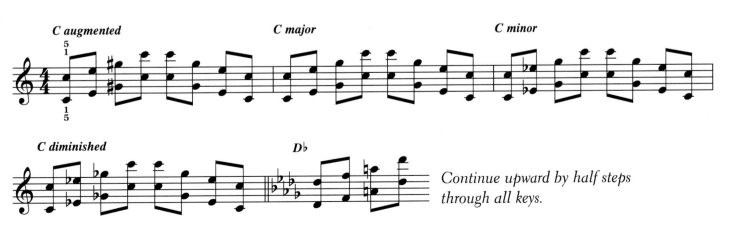

*Continue upward by half steps
through all keys.*

27 Broken Seventh Chords in Octaves (Major, Dominant, Minor, Half Diminished, Fully Diminished)

Play with one octave between the hands.

Continue upward by half steps through all keys.

28 Broken Chords and Arpeggios in Octaves

Franz Liszt (1811–1886)
from *Technical Exercises for the Piano*
"Broken Chords and Arpeggios in Octaves," Book XII, No. 84

Continue upward by half steps through all keys.

29 Octave Leaps

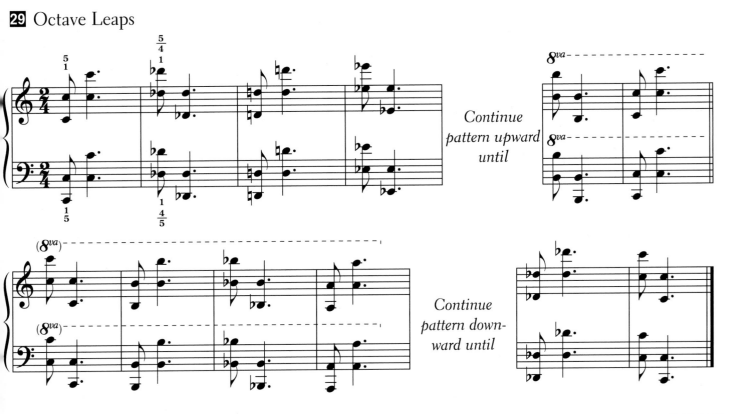

Continue pattern upward until

Continue pattern down-ward until

Part Seven ❦ Trills

Preparation

1 "Bird Calls"

Use different combinations of fingers 1-2, 2-3, 3-4, 4-5, 1-3, 2-4, 3-5.
Play LH one octave below RH.

2 "Add-On" Pattern

Feel the pulse. Use different combinations of fingers 1-2, 2-3, 3-4, 4-5, 1-3, 2-4, 3-5.
Play LH one octave below RH.

Starting on upper note

Continue as above

3 Shifting Accent

Play LH one octave below RH.

4 Exercise

Play LH one octave below RH.

Wolfgang Amadeus Mozart
(1756–1791)

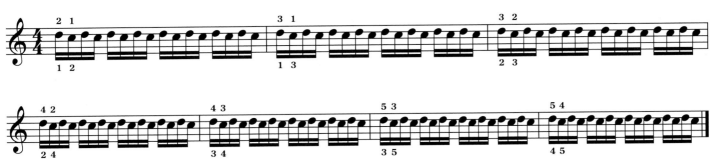

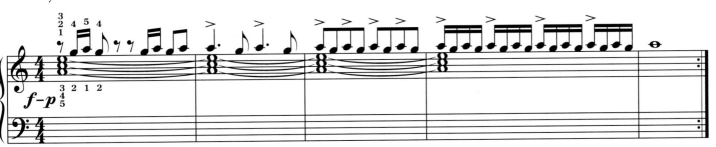

With Sustained Notes

Isidor Philipp (1863–1958)
from *Complete School of Technic for the Piano*
"Trills," No. 1

5

Play LH two octaves below RH.

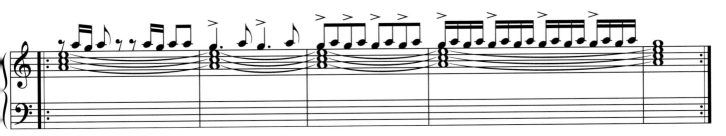

Note: For smaller hands, eliminate the bottom note of the triad (A); play C–E (RH 1-2, LH 5-4).

Isidor Philipp (1863–1958)
from *Complete School of Technic for the Piano*
"Trills," No. 14

6

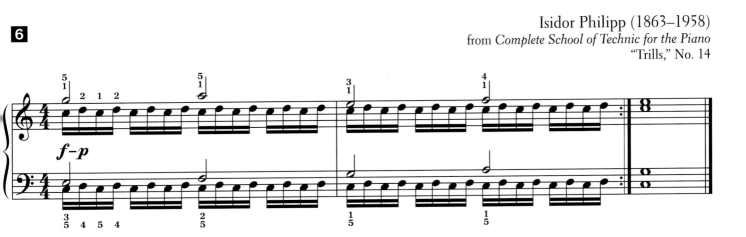

7 Study

Friedrich Wieck (1785–1873)
from *Pianoforte Studies*
"Study of the Trill with Sustained Notes," No. 43

8 Study

Friedrich Wieck (1785–1873)
from *Pianoforte Studies*
"Study of the Trill with Sustained Notes," No. 44

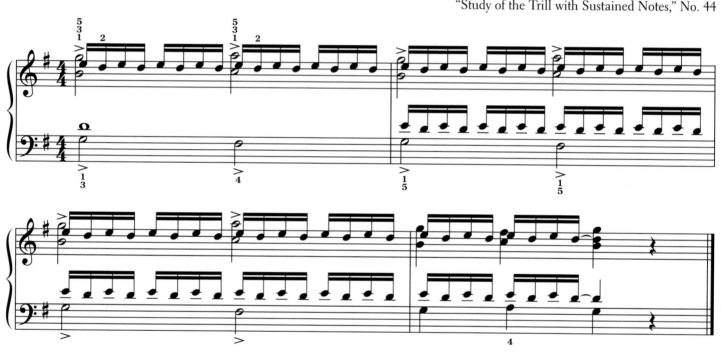

Double Thirds

9 Four-Note Trill in Thirds

Charles-Louis Hanon (1819–1900)
from *The Virtuoso Pianist in 60 Exercises*
Part 3, No. 54

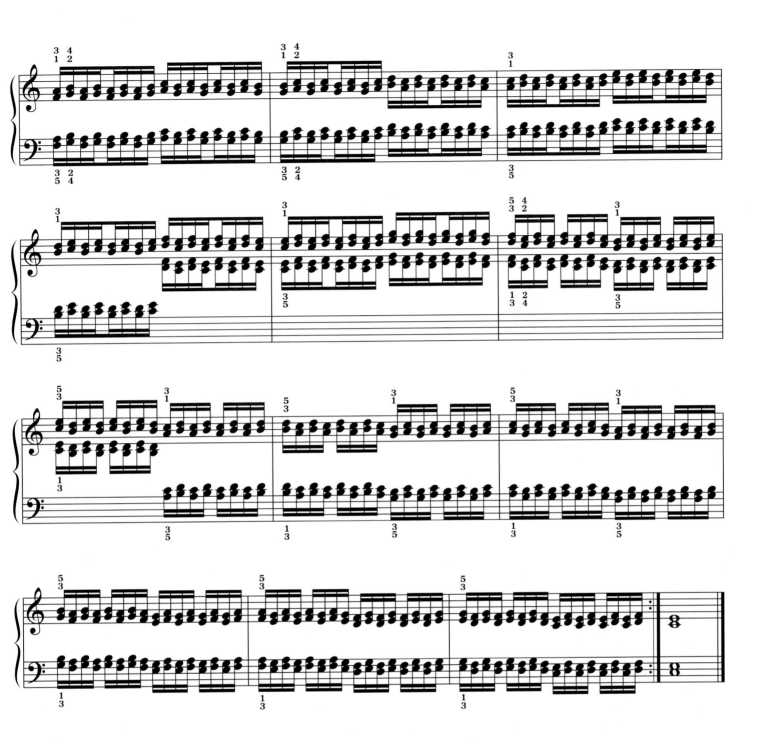

10 Double Thirds with Sustained Notes

Isidor Philipp (1863–1958)
from *Complete Scool of Technic for the Piano*
"Trills," No. 15

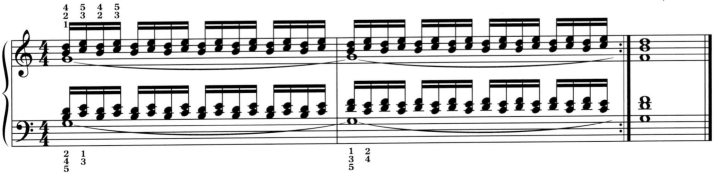

11 Double Thirds with Sustained Notes

Moritz Moszkowski (1854–1925)
from *School of Double Notes*, Op. 64, No. 11

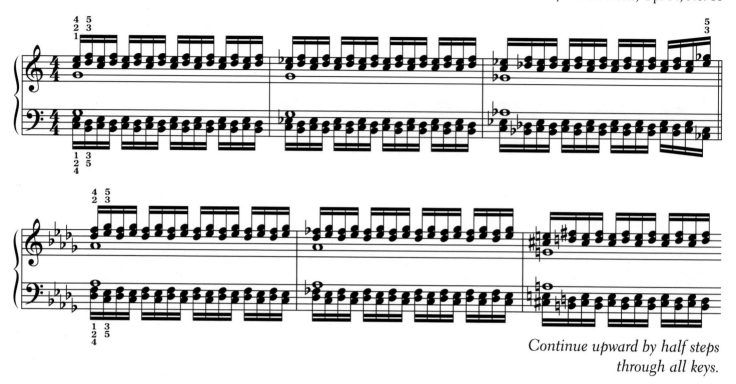

*Continue upward by half steps
through all keys.*

12 Double Thirds and Fourths with Sustained Notes

attr. to Sergei Rachmaninoff
(1873–1943)

a.

*Continue upward by half steps
through all keys.*

b.

*Continue upward by half steps
through all keys.*

Part Eight ❧ Repeated Notes

Groups of Two

1 Diatonic

Charles-Louis Hanon (1819–1900)
from *The Virtuoso Pianist in 60 Exercises*
Part 3, No. 45

Use different combinations of fingers 1-2, 2-3, 3-4, 4-5, 1-3, 2-4.

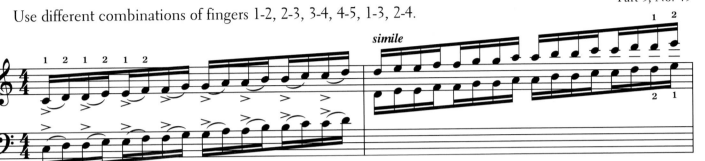

2 Chromatic

Use different combinations of fingers 1-2, 2-3, 3-4, 4-5, 1-3, 2-4.

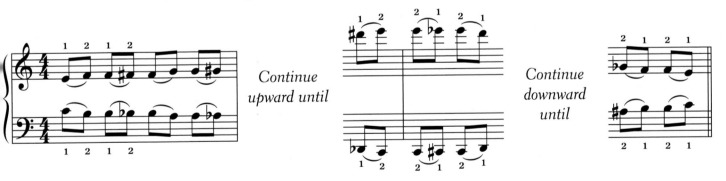

Continue
upward until

Continue
downward
until

Isidor Philipp (1863–1958)
from *Complete School of Technic for the Piano*
"Double Fourths," No. 1

3 Fourths

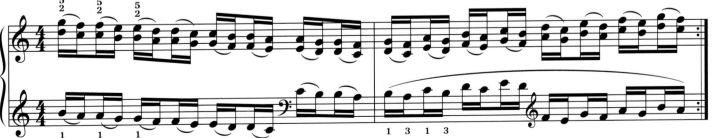

Double Notes

4 Detached Thirds

Charles-Louis Hanon (1819–1900)
from *The Virtuoso Pianist in 60 Exercises*
"Wrist Exercise Using Detached Thirds," Part 3, No. 48a
(Section A)

5 Detached Sixths

Charles-Louis Hanon (1819–1900)
from *The Virtuoso Pianist in 60 Exercises*
"Wrist Exercise Using Detached Sixths," Part 3, No. 48b
(Section A)

6 Octaves

Play with one octave between the hands.

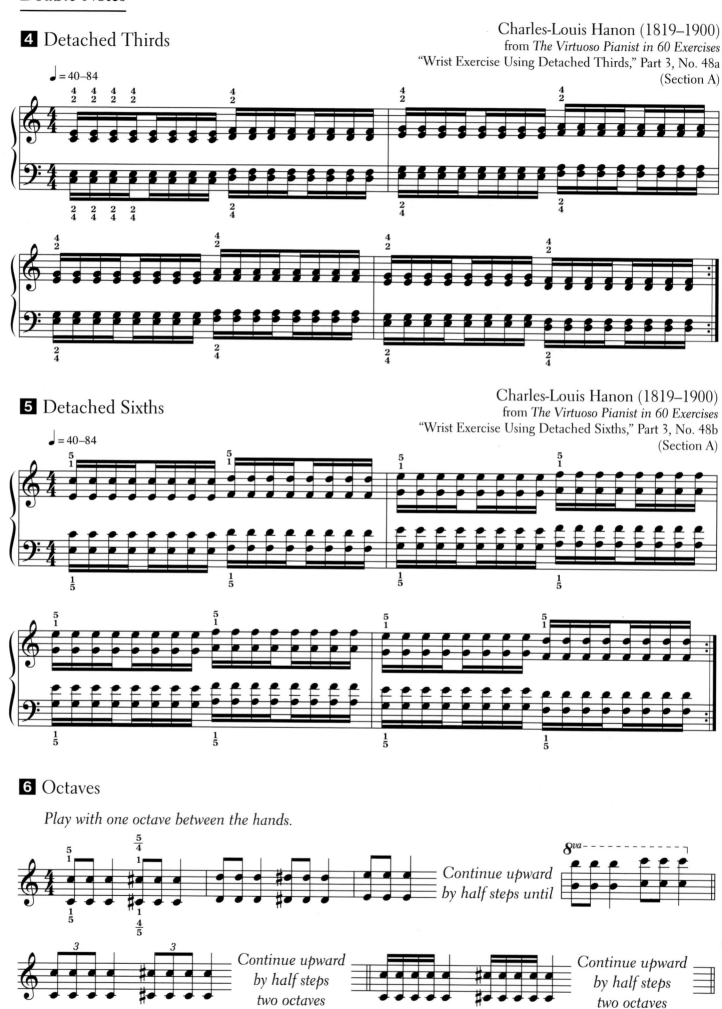

Continue upward
by half steps until

Continue upward
by half steps
two octaves

Continue upward
by half steps
two octaves

7 Etude in C Major

Carl Czerny (1791–1857)
from *Six Exercises des Octaves*, Op. 533, No. 1

Repeated Chords

8 Chords and Inversions

Franz Liszt (1811–1886)
from *Technical Exercises for the Piano*
"Repeated Chords and Inversions," Book I, No. 37

*Continue major-minor pattern
through all keys.*

9 Wrist Exercise

Rafael Joseffy (1852–1915)
from *School of Advanced Piano Playing*
"Repeated Chords. Wrist Exercises," Part 13a

*Continue upward by half steps
through all keys.*

10 With Sustained Octaves

Rafael Joseffy (1852–1915)
from *School of Advanced Piano Playing*
"Repeated Chords. Wrist Exercises," Part 13a

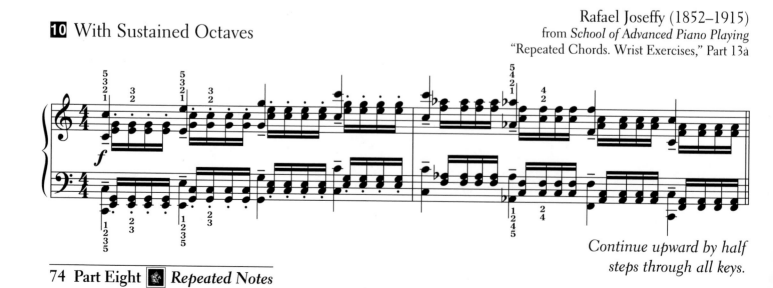

*Continue upward by half
steps through all keys.*

Prelude in B♭ Minor

Anatol Lyadov (1855–1914)
from *Preludes*, Op. 31, No. 2

With Changing Fingers

12 Etude in D Major

Muzio Clementi (1752–1832)
from *Gradus ad Parnassum*, No. 20

13 Changing Fingers 3-2-1

Isidor Philipp (1863–1958)
from *Complete School of Technic for the Piano*
"Repeated Notes," No. 1, Changing Fingers 3-2-1

14 Changing Fingers 4-3-2-1

Isidor Philipp (1863–1958)
from *Complete School of Technic for the Piano*
"Repeated Notes," No. 2, Changing Fingers 4-3-2-1

15 Changing Fingers 4-3-2-1

Friedrich Wieck (1785–1873)
from *Pianoforte Studies*
Changing Fingers 4-3-2-1, Section I, No. 56

Part Nine ✿ *Rotation*

Rafael Joseffy (1852–1915)
from *School of Advanced Piano Playing*
"Changing Fingers on One Key," Part 10

1 Changing Fingers on One Key

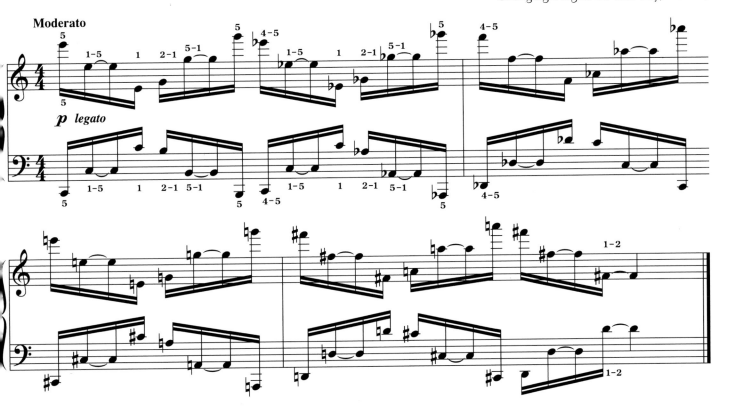

2 Contrary Motion

3 Parallel Motion

Play LH one or two octaves below RH.

4 Etude in G Major

Moritz Moszkowski (1854–1925)
from *20 Petite Etudes*, Op. 91, No. 1

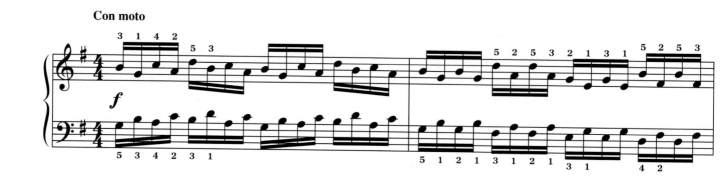

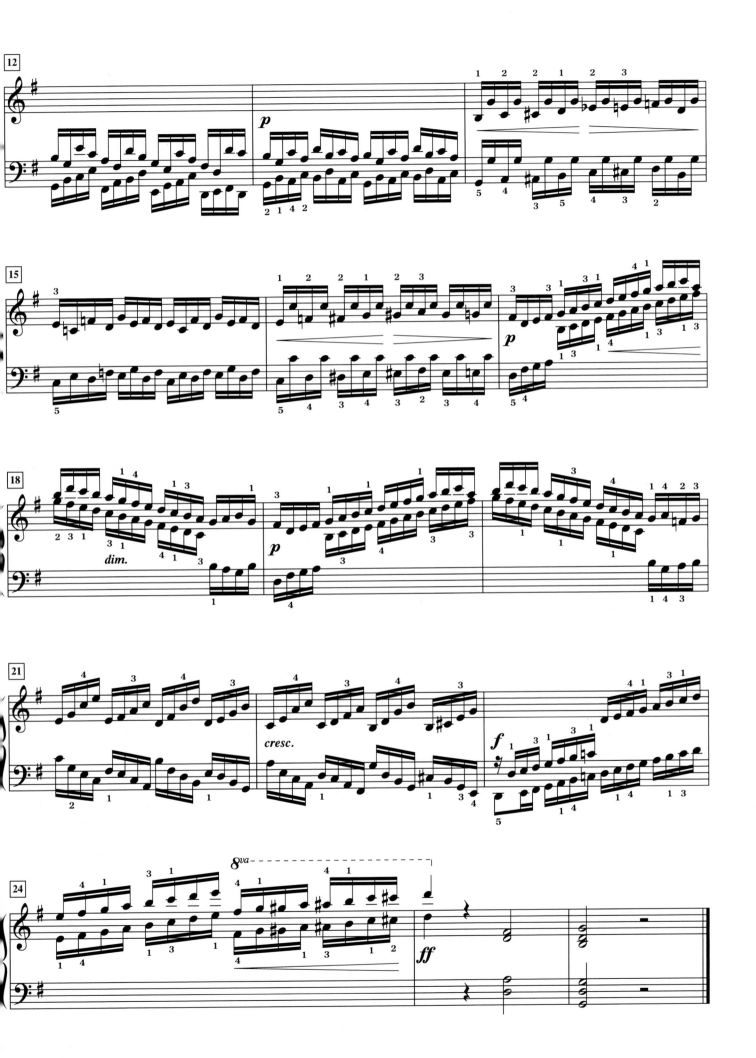

5 Study in C Major

Jean-Baptiste Duvernoy (1802–1880)
from *École du mécanisme*, Op. 120, No. 13

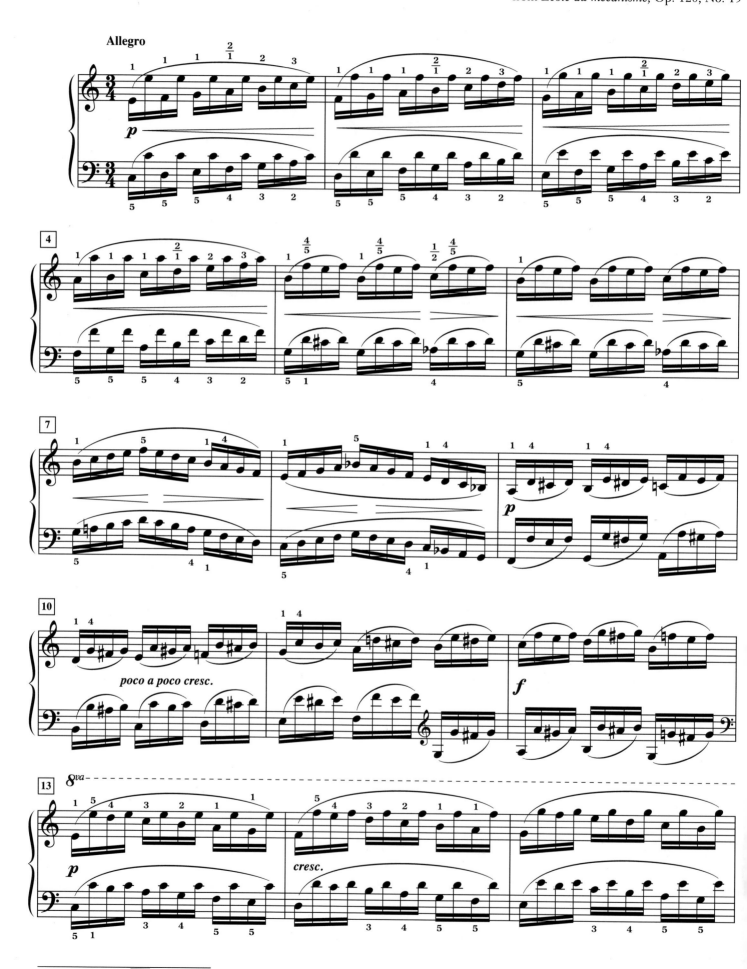

6 With Repeated Notes

Friedrich Wieck (1785–1873)
from *Pianoforte Studies*
Section I, No. 19

7 Contrary Motion

Carl Czerny (1791–1857)
from *160 Eight-Measure Exercises*, Op. 821, No. 88

Part Ten ❧ *Alternating Hands*

1 Single Notes

Isidor Philipp (1863–1958)
from *Complete School of Technic for the Piano*
"Linked Trill," No. 7

*Rests are not included with alternating 16th notes for ease in reading in this study
and similarly in studies 2, 3 and 5 below.

2 Single Notes

Alfred Cortot (1877–1962)
from *Rational Principles of Pianoforte Technique*
"Technique of the Wrist," (Alternating Hands), Chapter V, Series A, No. 4a

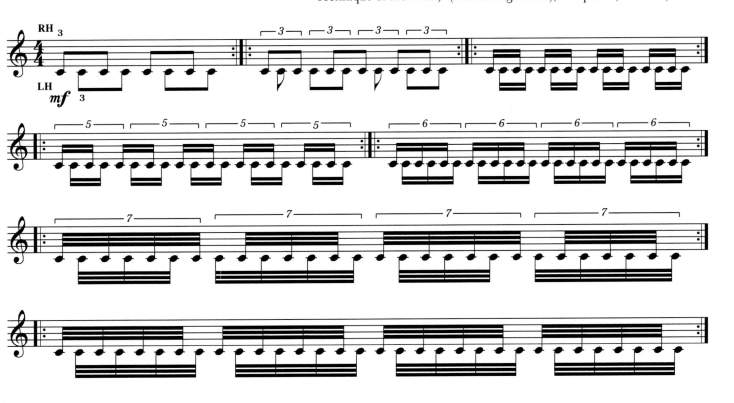

3 Double Notes—Thirds

Rafael Joseffy (1852–1915)
from *School of Advanced Piano Playing*
"Repetitions without Changing Fingers," Part 11a

4 Double Notes—Octaves

Transpose to all keys.

5 Octaves and Chords

Rafael Joseffy (1852–1915)
from *School of Advanced Piano Playing*
"Repetitions without Changing Fingers," Part 11

*Continue upward by half steps
through all keys.*

6 Study in A Minor

Ludvig Schytte (1848–1909)
from 25 *Melodious Studies*, Op. 108, No. 5

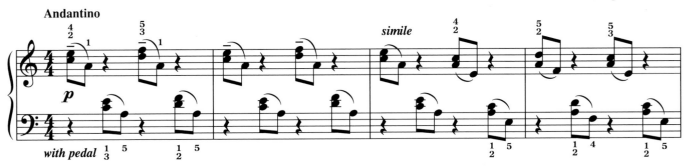

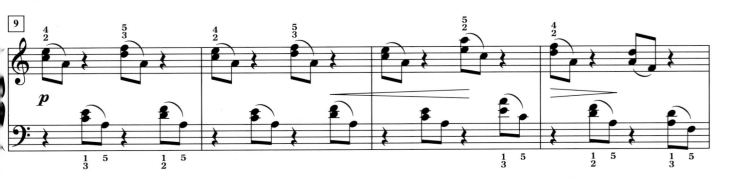

7 Study in B♭ Major

Anatol Lyadov (1855–1914)
from *Biroulki (Young People's Games)*, Op. 2, No. 12

8 Etude of Alternating Double Notes—Confetti

Donald Waxman (b. 1925)
from *50 Etudes*, Vol. II, No. 19

Carl Czerny (1791–1857)
from *160 Eight-Measure Exercises*, Op. 821, No. 98

Part Eleven ❧ *Chromatic Patterns*

1 Minor Thirds

Charles-Louis Hanon (1819–1900)
from *The Virtuoso Pianist in 60 Exercises*
Part 3, No. 50

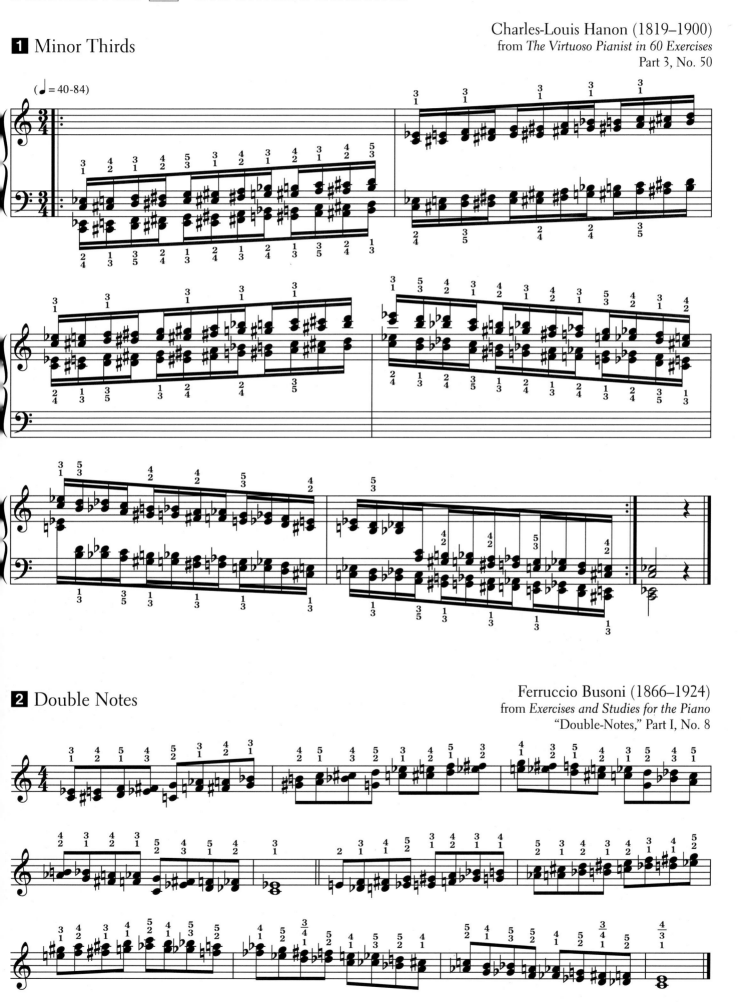

2 Double Notes

Ferruccio Busoni (1866–1924)
from *Exercises and Studies for the Piano*
"Double-Notes," Part I, No. 8

3 Study in F Major

Felix Le Couppey (1811–1887)
from *L'Agilité*, Op. 20, No. 23

4 With Sustained Notes

Friedrich Wieck (1785–1873)
from *Pianoforte Studies*
Section I, No. 45

5 Legato Octaves

Play with one octave between the hands.

Isidor Philipp (1863–1958)
from *Complete School of Technic for the Piano*
"Legato Octaves," No. 4